Interview

EXPRESS

Interview Express

Interview

EXPRESS

Know How to Prepare for an Interview and Ace It to Get a Job

Daniel Wells & KnowIt Express

N2K Publication

ISBN 978-1-533-46571-9

Printed in the United States of America

First Edition

Welcome to the *Know It Express* - the express lane to knowledge!

To stay up-to-date, please be sure to sign up for **our newsletter** at http://www.KnowItExpress.com and follow us on social media:

https://www.facebook.com/KnowItExpress
https://twitter.com/KnowItExpress
https://plus.google.com/+KnowItExpress

EXPRESS LANE

Interview Express

CHAPTER 1

Unraveling the Mysterious Battle Ahead

The Twilight Zone

The concept of an **interview** needs no introduction. And yet, it's *not easy to figure out* how to interview **well**. Years of research and hundreds of tips and techniques later, the essence of what constitutes the PERFECT interview remains a *mystery*.

- Have you had an interview before? Do you still recall the interview(s) at which you were successful?

Did you prepare, or were you trying to be spontaneous?

- Do you recall an interview that did NOT go so well? You may be able to pinpoint the exact moment when things started to fall apart.

There are many different types of interviews, and unless you're living under a rock, chances are you will be subjected to some kind of interview sooner or later.

So for your next interview, do you have a game plan in mind or do you wanna wing it? Whatever you choose, you're probably going to pick a style that you *think* will help you succeed. *But will it?*

Is there a **winning equation** or a **secret code,** a sure shot technique that will lead to a successful interview? Well, perhaps buried in a pot of gold at the end of a rainbow...but until then, let's figure out this treasure map. While there is no magic formula, there are some strategies that will put you on the road to success.

The Black Hole Called 'Interview'

When you look at the big picture, recruitment processes are pretty routine. They are predictable, sequential, and conditional. No matter what other components are added, such as tests (logical, psychological, physical, aptitude), group discussions, auditions, etc., the 'interview' remains a standard feature.

If you've been interviewed before, you're already aware that it's pretty much a <u>one-sided conversation</u> where you answer a **ton of questions**. At the end of it, you hope for the best, but it can be hard to tell what went well or where you slipped up.

It's a bit like being a patient undergoing a surgery: you're going through the procedure, without having any insight into its technicalities, and are completely at the mercy of the experts.

It is an *opaque process;* you can do your best and still not know if you passed or not!

When they don't pass, some people go looking for feedback but by this point even "American Idol" does a better job of giving feedback and reasoning behind their judgment.

The Pandemonium Called 'Process'

To *train* the beast, you must *understand* the beast. So let's start peeling away the layers to find ways to increase your chances at successfully **cracking an interview**.

Recruitment is all about **standardization**. Providing a 'level playing field' for all candidates, and then finding who performs the best.

First among equals.

For any legal employment where you will eventually fill out some type of IRS form, the law requires the process to be compliant, i.e. to conform to the following standards.

- The recruitment process be free from all sorts of discrimination of race, color, national origin, religion, gender, age, disability, genetic information, or reprisal.

- The job description must list basic qualifications required for a person to perform this role effectively.

- Each candidate must be evaluated using the same process and based on the same set of basic qualifications.

- ALL candidates interviewed or hired for the job must meet or exceed the basic qualifications.

There are also a few other technical regulations that we won't go into here (minimum number of days for job advertising, documentation, working with other 'agencies', etc.).

So yes, there is a "recruitment process." Yes, there are tools used in the process.

But all of these processes, at the end of the day, are subservient to the subjective evaluation and decision of a small group of people—**the interviewers.**

CHAPTER 2

The Battle Has Just Begun

Devise A New Plan of Attack

Have you ever felt that you were **fully qualified** for a job and that the role description and the qualifications were actually describing you, only to wait for weeks—or even months—after applying to hear anything?

You wait.

And wait.

And nothing. No calls from the company after a measly automatic reply.

This is the fate of thousands, if not millions, of applications every day.

But this is a passive way to look for a job, people say to you. **Network.** *Yes! That's the secret.* Then you connect with folks on LinkedIn, reconnect with old acquaintances and associates...and in general follow the networking guidelines.

But you're still miles away from the possibility of an interview.

What is a worthy job seeker to do?

Exercise: Recruit Allies

While you are working on your networking, here is an important tip that could save a ton of heartburn: **DO NOT** approach the human resources person as your first step.

Yup, you heard that right!

<u>Step 1</u>: **Find a resource** - If you see a job that you're interested in, before applying, look for people who may be associated with that role—managers, other team members, previous employees—and any other possible connections you may already have with the company.

<u>Step 2</u>: **Build a context** - Reach out to a couple of these folks who will understand your skills—the ones in your field who would understand the contribution you can make or the potential you have. Introduce yourself (through email or LinkedIn) and express interest in the position. Ask if they can refer you to the hiring manager or recruiter.

Ever wonder what a blockbuster, Oscar-winning Hollywood film would look like if all the people working on that project were recruited by an HR person?

That's why it is important to connect with folks who can appreciate your expertise *before* going through "the process."

Once your résumé gets enough eyeballs from the right people, you will be invited for the first interview.

<u>Exercise</u>: Live To Fight Another Day

The recruitment 'process' is the company's way of preparing. They don't reach out without preparation, and you shouldn't either.

So the next time you get a call to interview, make sure you do the following:

1.) DO NOT accept an **impromptu interview**, even on the phone! If the person asks to "take a few minutes," politely tell them that you have something scheduled within the next 10 minutes and will have to reschedule. Tell them that you want to be fully available and prepared for the discussion, whether it's by phone or in-person.

2.) When scheduling the interview, ask questions that will help you plan and prepare.

- *"How much time should I schedule for this discussion?"* – Not only will this help you schedule your time (remember to add transportation time and another 30 minutes in case it goes overtime), it will also give you a sense for how in depth the interview will be.

- *"Who is the interviewer? Is this person the direct manager for this position?"* – Get that person's information, if possible, so that you can look them up on LinkedIn or ask people in your network. This will also help you determine what kind of boss you might have at this job.

- *"Why is the position open?"* – Expectations, challenges, and pressure will vary depending on if this is a new position and if the previous employee was successful or not.

- *"Can you please explain what the hiring process will be for this position and if you have any time frame in mind for completing the hire?"* – This will reduce the number of surprises for you and give you a better idea of what to expect.

3.) Confirm, thank, and close – Reconfirm the interview date, specifically mention the name of the interviewer, and say that you're looking forward to the discussion. Now that the person has spent time answering your questions, it'd be a good idea to thank them too.

CHAPTER 3

Training the Mightiest Warriors

You're In The Pool Now

For an interview, you only get <u>one shot</u> to get it right. Like the Wimbledon Tennis Grand Slam, you lose once and you're out.

You will need to succeed under pressure. You probably won't know much about the interviewers you'll be facing or the other candidates you'll be competing against. You will have to juggle the different personalities of the interviewers, answer questions like a master craftsman, and create a strong impression that knocks their socks off!

Getting an opportunity to interview is a very **small part** of the entire process. There are a bunch of reasons WHY you might have been *invited to interview* in the first place, and there is still a lot of work that will go into finally joining the team.

By the time you've been invited for the interview, it isn't about basic competence anymore...that's a given. *It's assumed.*

Here is what you need to understand about getting that call for an interview:

1.) You're **qualified**. Of course! Otherwise they wouldn't bother calling you.

2.) You've been **noticed**. Something in your application—whether your school, your experience, your previous employers, your recommendations, or your results—was noticed!

3.) You have **potential**—the ability to do the job. That's why they are interested in hearing what you have to say.

4.) You have the **opportunity** to be hired.

That said, clearly it's now time to *get serious and prepare*!

<u>News Flash</u>: Amateurs aren't drafted for the NFL, strong professionals are. So spontaneity is NOT the key. Rigor is. Do the hard work, stay focused, and stay determined.

<u>Exercise</u>: You've Shown Great Potential

Why me? Just like the American penal system (the judicial courts), which says *you're innocent until proven guilty*, in the interview process, you're *qualified until proven unsuitable*. So far so good, don't mess it up!

Step-1 Job description review: Read the job description carefully and make a list of all the skills or qualifications that you fulfill and what you lack. (Yes, it's okay to lack some of the "preferred requirements" so long as you have the basics covered.)

Step-2 Résumé review: Read your résumé carefully and make a list of all the skills or qualifications that will enable you to succeed in this role.

Step-3 Compare: This is a simple exercise but is ignored by many candidates. Compare your résumé with the job description and find the key areas of alignment. Keep this list in mind as you move through the process. This is your success-list.

Step-4 Compare again: Make a list of the areas of disconnect—the skills and/or experience required or preferred that you don't have. This will help you foresee the challenging questions. This is your snag-list.

Finally, integrate the lists: For every objection or concern that is raised you will be able to offer a relevant strength that you bring to the role. For example, *I have not done 'this' before, however, I do have experience in 'that area,' so I will be able to utilize my skills to learn and perform 'this.'*

Exercise: Don't Reveal Your Poison

To put it bluntly, your **social media** can kill your career.

Our lives are entirely online now. Where we live, who we date, pictures from our vacations, college degrees, relationship status, names of our kids, restaurants we checked-in at, previous jobs and employers, family ancestry, criminal records, credit history...everything. And employers are looking at it.

Not only can your social media information **disqualify** you, it can also make you very vulnerable to strong negative backlash.

As part of your job search, clean up your social media.

Take stock of your accounts. Wherever possible, delete controversial content, remove objectionable photos, and become *aware* of all activities affecting your social media behavior.

<u>You're not in college anymore</u>. That photo of you passing out at a fraternity animal house party may have been a great laugh for a while...but employers **are not laughing**.

CHAPTER 4

Preparing for Battle

The Battle Is Won Before It Is Fought

What will they ask you? There is a **job scope**, but very little (except for topics protected by discrimination legislation, as discussed above) is off the table at an interview. Questions will be asked not only to check your *technical know-how* but also to uncover your *attitude* or *style of thinking*.

Skilled interviewers will easily <u>combine</u> behavioral elements in technical questions, and your answers to these questions sometimes say a lot more to them than anything else.

So do your research about the role, the company, and the industry in general. *That's a no-brainer.* The more you research, the more information you'll have. The consolidation and presentation of this information is key.

That's where **preparation** delivers results.

While one can't predict interview questions, certain types of questions should be expected. For example:

- Tell us something about yourself.

- Summarize your strengths and areas that could use improvement.

- Why do you want this job or to work at this company?

- Tell us about a challenging time when you succeeded.

- Tell us about a time when you failed.

- Talk about the time when you exhibited situational leadership, quick thinking, customer service, etc. (or any other relevant soft skill).

- How do you plan to succeed in this role?

- Why do you think we should hire you?

- What previous experience do you have in working with XYZ (add technical skills here)?

Exercise: The Ideal Solider

If *you were* the hiring manager for this role, what kind of employee would you want to hire? What questions would you ask the candidates, and how would you compare them?

What will the hiring manager be looking for? This is the key. Be your own audience!

1.) Make your list of top 10 expected questions and ideal responses for each.

2.) Make a list of the 5 toughest questions you're going to face and the ideal responses for each.

3.) Pick 2-4 real situations where you were at your best. Customize the narration of each "situation" for different themes—challenge, excellence at workplace, delivering to objectives, utilizing your skills, etc. Use these situations in your interview.

<u>Exercise</u>: A Rising Star

Over-preparation for an interview is not a sin. Sometimes you can use the same answer for a few similar questions. So rehearse.

Consider following the <u>STAR technique</u> to respond to behavioral questions. We recommend it because it is both concise and comprehensive:

1.) Situation at hand.

2.) Task to be done or objectives to be met.

3.) Actions taken by you—highlight the ones that reflect soft & technical skills.

4.) Results achieved due to your actions.

This method will help you deliver clear answers to their questions, no matter what they ask you!

CHAPTER 5

Know Thy Enemies and Obstacles

Play To The Team, Not A One-Man-Army

Too many candidates are *too focused* on their résumé. This takes them away from a **larger perspective**. They become so absorbed in talking about their own suitability for the job that they forget that this job is just one of the cogs in the wheel.

Zoom out people. Think about the **other people** who you would interact with in this position—team members, managers, other collaborators in the company, vendors, consultants, customers, partners, and even competitors.

Earlier, we told you about **competence** being the <u>common denominator</u> for the **candidates** in the pipeline.

- So what differentiates one candidate from the other? What is the hiring manager looking for?

<u>The answer</u> is simple—the company is looking for someone who *fits in their current environment.*

Your role will not function in solitude or in a vacuum. It will both affect and be affected by multiple stakeholders. And that's the mystery you need to solve for them during the interview: how will you influence others and how will you be influenced.

<u>Exercise</u>: Behind Enemy Lines

Yes, you've made a lot of lists by now: lists of questions, answers, skills, ideas, and more. Now evaluate each point to answer this question: so now what?

When you relate each of your questions and answers to a company situation (even hypothetical), you will drive home the message about job-fit.

Read the job description carefully, and you will find clues about the "responsibilities" and how these "responsibilities" interact with other roles.

Connect the dots. Remember, think as a **hiring manager**, not as a candidate.

What are they looking for?

Own Your Failures

The importance of **preparation, perspective** and **presentation** cannot be stressed enough. An interview is like a court hearing—you will be judged.

And you know how THAT feels...being judged.

When you're being asked to revisit your failures and your past stumbling blocks, it's not going to be easy. Actually, it's going to be as comfortable as a root canal.

Whether you like it or not, the interviewers will try to look for the <u>weak spots</u> in your background and experience, put you in a spot, and try to knock you down, *just to see how well you hold up*. They want to find the holes where your experience is not solid and to see how you handle the pressure.

Because they have other candidates to interview, they are looking for any excuse to disqualify you immediately and move on to the next. Don't make this easy for them.

Hence the emphasis on preparation, perspective, and presentation

Exercise: Consolidate And Integrate

Expect that you will face challenging questions during the interview that will make you nervous. It's okay. Remember, you're here—interviewing—at the right time, in the right place.

Preparation is expecting, solving, planning, and arranging your content.

1.) Expect tough questions and to be cornered. Prepare your answers.

2.) Expect 'problem statements.' (Example: "This role requires it but you don't have any experience with xyz.") Prepare your solution.

3.) Expect future-oriented questions. (<u>Example</u>: "What steps would you take to succeed in this area?") Foresee, think, and prepare your plan.

4.) There is a lot of information that you want to present and they want to know. Consolidate your thoughts as per priority and impact. Prepare concise answers.

Perspective is one of the most important aspects frequently neglected by candidates. The interviewer is looking for context with which to understand you better.

1.) When preparing an answer make sure you briefly explain two different or even opposing points-of-view. (<u>Example</u>: "While I had to follow all compliance guidelines, it was understandable that the customer was getting increasingly frustrated with our processes.")

2.) When talking about successes, don't forget to mention the challenges and failures that led to the success. This enables empathy and is much more powerful than a success out of context.

3.) When talking about failures, ALWAYS talk about what you learned from it and the effort towards attaining a stretched goal. Take responsibility for the failure.

4.) When describing an achievement, acknowledge the people associated with this success. Not sharing credit will come across as gloating and will be off-putting. But also explain your role in it.

Presentation is everything! At the end of the day, your book *will be judged* by its cover.

1.) Be thorough and clear in the delivery of your answers.

2.) Smile, make eye contact, and stay relaxed.

3.) Use humor carefully and sparingly.

CHAPTER 6

Attacking the Interview

On Judgment Day

So here you are, at the interview. *It's the moment of truth.*

You'll be surprised by how difficult it is to come across as both smart and "normal" during an interview. If you under-interview, you will likely come across as inadequate, but if you over-interview, you may come across as too arrogant.

You'll probably be a nervous wreck *inside* your skin, but never mind…put your game face on and dive in! This is your obstacle course so do everything you can to <u>keep it simple</u>.

Besides all the preparation that you've walked in with, here are some pointers:

- **Carry a neutral personality.** The interviewers are allowed to be extreme in their opinions, observations, and expressions. <u>You are not</u>. Don't slip into informality, even if the interviewer does. This is not a time to develop a friendship or act like chums!

- **Q&A - Get to the point!** This is no time for storytelling. Be <u>professional</u> in your responses and use an appropriate level of enthusiasm. Leave out urban slang and stick to your prepared responses where they are relevant. (If they throw a curveball at you, remember the STAR method.)

- **Mind your manners.** Put your best foot forward: do not interrupt or speak out of turn, use a polite tone and volume, mind your 'please' and 'thank-yous', smile appropriately, don't stare, and basically don't do <u>anything</u> that will make you look like a complete jerk!

- **Unwrap the job.** Ask questions about the job <u>specifics</u> so that you understand the kind of person they are looking for (but not anything you could be expected to have read yourself on their website).

- **"Fit for the job?"** Stay within the normal curve. That doesn't mean you should be mediocre, but stay away from extremes and make sure they know you will be reliable. Surprises are rarely favorable.

- **Follow up.** Always close the loop. Reassert your interest in the position, and thank interviewers for the opportunity to interview.

If this feels like too many things to remember, consider this simplification: the hiring managers want to know whether they are making the **right decision** by hiring YOU. And there are many ways you can sabotage your own chances if you're *not* self-aware. So be aware.

Do NOT Be Yourself

Now if you get too nervous and forget all your pointers, just remember one simple rule: DO NOT be yourself!

- **DO NOT be yourself!** An interview is not a time to be casual or cool! Be professional. 'They' want to know if you can do the job well and if you will make a trustworthy and stable employee. Your objective is to highlight your relevant experience and skills.

- **DO NOT be yourself!** An interview is not speed dating. This is no time to reveal your hobbies, the story behind your tattoos, how you've relocated to follow the love of your life, how you have to sell the house to pay for a divorce, or anything else about your personal life. Bottle up the stories and emotions, and keep all your answers on-point.

- **DO NOT be yourself!** Keep your opinions to yourself and avoid taking-a-stand. You may win the argument but lose the opportunity. Pick your battles and stay away from controversial comments. Balance is key. Stay neutral.

<u>Exercise</u>: Fight With Style

Have *someone else* dress you up for the interview.

Find a good friend or family member with an understanding of workplace attire. (Parents are a great resource here!) Invite your confidant to your closet, and **together** you can decide on a polished, professional outfit.

Also have a **plan-B outfit** ready in case of mishaps such as coffee spills. Keep a second set of clothes (and accessories) ready-to-go should you be caught in a Murphy's law situation.

<u>Exercise</u>: The Final Attack

Lower the stress and up the confidence.

Take serious steps to **reduce your stress**. Build structure and predictability or develop a comfort zone...whatever works for you. If you can, talk to a mentor or friend who can <u>give you a pep talk</u>. And then find a way to *distract* yourself in the moments before the interview. Listen to music or read a book.

For the day of your interview, keep an open calendar. Try to get some good sleep, and then line up your **'favorites'** during the day: get your favorite drink from Starbucks, play your favorite music in the car, eat your favorite comfort food...whatever settles your nerves.

When you start looking for a job, you start preparing your toolbox. Here's what you're going to need to keep your stress low and your confidence stable:

1.) **Kick-ass résumé** – clear, neat, bulleted, concise, and certainly without typos (have someone else look it over). Focus on results and not just tasks.

2.) **Cheat sheet** – questions you will ask, quotes/jokes you will use, examples you will give, etc. Read it quickly, just before your interview, to have some key points ready.

3.) **Strong references** – talk to your references and prep them about the role you are applying for.

4.) **Checklist** – what you will wear, eat, documents to carry, map...anything you might need.

CHAPTER 7

Trials Coming to a Close

You Win Some, You Lose Some

Super Mario was super because he had <u>3 lives</u>, collected brownie points along the way, and could see what's coming. You are not super Mario. :) So there is a lot of pressure to *get it right* the first time, or else you're out!

Interviewing is a *nerve-wracking* process; it is a **test**. It challenges everyone and even the best fail at it <u>multiple times</u>.

Failing an interview is an **opportunity** to learn and continue hunting. It is not necessarily a reflection on your quality as professional or even your interview skills. Sometimes there's just a better candidate in pool or the funding falls through and no one is hired at all.

Interviews are about comparing a handful of qualified individuals and figuring out who will be the **most suitable for the company**. It's important to understand that candidates are selected for a variety of reasons other than the fact that they are qualified (which is a given).

But if you've gotten this far, you're already starting to prepare for your success in the upcoming interview, and there is no better time for preparation than NOW.

Ace In The Hole

While they seem daunting, interviews are not that difficult to handle. Here's a <u>final list of tips</u> for you:

1.) Minutes before the interview, take deep **breaths**, stand or sit *confidently*, and clear your head.

2.) Use **affirmations** to calm your nerves and strengthen your confidence.

3.) During and after the interview, remember to give yourself **positive** energy. Be *optimistic* about opportunities that lie ahead and be at peace with the efforts you've made.

5.) Send thank-you notes (written or emailed) to the people you met. Be genuine, not desperate, in expressing gratitude.

5.) Objectively review your interview experience and, if required, **update** your game plan or notes for the next interview.

6.) Avoid obsessing over the discussion and consciously *let go of the restlessness*.

7.) If you have not received any news after the interview, **follow up** with the relevant staff in a few days and reassert your interest in the position. If you have received communication, send <u>another thank-you note</u>.

You never really know how an interview is going to turn out and can never tell if you've made it. But you always know if you've **given it your best**.

So if you want to be drafted...train hard, play strong, and hit them with your best shot.

You can do this!

"You miss 100% of the shots you don't take."
- **Wayne Gretzky**

Interview Express

Now You Know!

We have now gone from - *NOT knowing*...to *KNOWING*.

Doesn't it feel great? As cliché as the proverbial saying goes: knowledge is, indeed, power. The more you know, the more empowered you become. Not knowing is defeating, as you succumb to feelings of helplessness and surrendering of your own self.

Of course, acquiring knowledge is a never-ending quest. There is a great saying by Nobel Prize French author Andre Gide: "Believe those who are seeking the truth. Doubt those who find it."

At the very least, we hope we have set you off in the right path in regards to what you have set out to know, and that you have enjoyed our little journey together for the time you have spent with us.

If you can tell us how we did, that would be very appreciated! We value your feedback and always look forward to hearing from you, or if there is any way we could improve the entire experience for you. If you have a success story, even better - please let us know!

http://www.KnowItExpress.com

Don't forget to stay in contact for we would love to connect with you.

https://www.facebook.com/KnowItExpress
https://twitter.com/KnowItExpress
https://plus.google.com/+KnowItExpress

What would you like to know? Let us know!

CONTACT US

Now onward for more power to you, and thank you!

www.ingramcontent.com/pod-product-compliance
Lightning Source LLC
Chambersburg PA
CBHW030703190526
45164CB00004B/368